T0049345

HAUS CURIOSITIES

The Vitality of Democracy

About the Author

Gisela Stuart was the Labour MP for Birmingham Edgbaston from 1997 to 2017 and a minister in Tony Blair's government. She chaired Vote Leave in the 2016 referendum on the United Kingdom's continued membership of the European Union. In 2020 she joined the House of Lords as a crossbench peer, and in 2022 she was appointed as the First Civil Service Commissioner.

Gisela Stuart

THE VITALITY OF DEMOCRACY

First published by Haus Publishing in 2022
4 Cinnamon Row
London SW11 3TW
www.hauspublishing.com

A CIP catalogue record for this book is
available from the British Library

Print ISBN: 978-1-913368-51-7
Ebook ISBN: 978-1-913368-52-4

Typeset in Garamond by MacGuru Ltd

Printed in the United Kingdom

Contents

Introduction

We, the people, are the inhabitants of a light blue dot in the red spectrum, part of an ever-expanding, seemingly limitless universe. On this, our planet, we have increased in number, transformed and consumed more and more of its natural resources, and at times even believed that we were the masters of the universe.

We created enduring works of art and beauty, behaved with unspeakable cruelty, articulated profound truths, and made stunning discoveries. In our world, the one that we have shaped, we believe progress to be inevitable. Anything that would suggest otherwise we treat as no more than a setback. Standing still is not an option. We learnt early on that families and being part of a group make us stronger, and our need for identity, belonging, and community has remained with us ever since. We developed and adapted institutions and created ever-larger and more complex systems. When we encountered constraints or threats, we came up with technical solutions based on enlightenment principles, science, and engineering.

And yet, to this day, no one really knows how to run society. There are no fixed rules, natural laws, or reliable laboratory tests. It is a system of trial and error. We try to do our best at any given time. When we encounter something unexpected, we know that the solution lies in allowing for doubt and acknowledging that there is much we don't yet know. Some new ideas will work, others will not. Progress demands failure as well as success.

This does not mean that there are no fundamental principles underpinning the choices we make and the structures we choose. They are not fixed and will change over time, but they are essential guiding principles. They ought to ensure that we don't lose our way.

In the United Kingdom, we live in a liberal democracy. We take pride in that. We believe and hope that, given the choice and opportunity, everyone would want to live in a society like ours. There was a time, not so long ago, when we thought we had reached a tipping point. Tyrants, autocrats, and repressors had had their day. Only social markets and democracy could deliver liberty, economic prosperity, and security. Our system of government, in the hands of the many and not the few, would be so attractive that it would simply spread and quite naturally prevail.

It hasn't quite worked out like that. In 2021, less than half of the world's population lived in a democracy of some sort, and the figure is declining. Established democracies are becoming complacent, whilst authoritarian regimes are turning more aggressive.

We moved away from accepting some higher authorities. No longer would gods or monarchs determine matters of state without constraint. We required those in authority to be mandated by those who are being governed. No one was to be exempt from the rule of law. Everyone of a certain age would have a vote. We did want our leaders to be people like us, but not all the time. When the situation demanded it, we expected them to be wise, display fortitude, have a strong moral compass, and above all be able to make decisions under pressure.

As we were entrenching freedom of speech and the right to express our own preferences and opinions, we started to forget that there was also a responsibility to listen to others. Few decisions are ideal for everyone, but they can be right if they serve the wider interests of the community. Things would be easier if there were such a thing as a perfect answer, but there isn't. In a democracy, the integrity of the process of arriving at a decision is just as important as the decision itself. It requires compromises and trade-offs, the need to respect minorities, as well as accepting responsibility for the result. And to top it all, there must be a willingness to review and adapt in the light of changing circumstances and public sentiments.

This is not to deny the human desire to want to know what happens next. We all want certainty and security and would like to think that someone somewhere has all the answers. But life isn't like that.

Governments should do the big things that individuals and small communities can't do. Defence, national infrastructure, and welfare to name a few. We expect them to prevent bad things from happening, even if we rarely give them credit for it when they succeed. Come election time, showing off a shiny new hospital is always more impressive than standing on a soapbox explaining that because we passed laws to reduce smoking, enabled everyone to walk more and take regular exercise, and expanded health screening programmes we don't need a new hospital. That's just how it is. It does not excuse government from not doing the big important things. There may not be many votes in building flood barriers, but government is quite rightly blamed when there are heavy rains and rivers overflow, bringing misery to thousands of people. Governing is easy for democrats as well as autocrats when the economy is growing and there are plenty of good things to be handed out. It's much harder when they have to cut spending, curtail freedoms, and increase taxes.

And then comes the day when a discussion about whether a butterfly flapping its wings in New Mexico really has the power to cause an earthquake in China isn't just a moot point in a lecture on chaos theory. It is the day when, as a consequence of something that happened to a bat in Wuhan, we are all told to stay at home, close our schools and borders, and start every day with a counting of the number of people who have died at home and abroad.

Governments are asked to respond to something they have never dealt with before. There are models of what might happen next, but no one can say for sure. We use the language of war, but you can't negotiate with a mutating virus. Individual freedoms and liberties are curtailed in the interest of the national as well as the global good. Every single government responds differently. All make mistakes at some point or another.

The lives of citizens are controlled by their democratic governments in a manner unprecedented in peace time, from data collection for vaccinations to apps that track their movements and identify close contacts. At a time when democracy is under threat around the world, now is a suitable moment to reflect on what democracy means, what makes the system work, and what is required to ensure its enduring vitality.

Setting the Scene

We live in families, communities, and nations. Most of the important things in life can only be achieved collectively. Once we have dealt with existential threats and moved beyond immediate demands and obligations, we need ideals, beliefs, and principles that underpin the decisions and choices we make in our daily lives.

There was a time when the fate of humans was in the hands of a multitude of deities. Much of Europe then moved towards giving the last word to just one god. Priests mediated between God and man. Monarchs, anointed by God, led the nation. God was all-powerful and his message was 'Be still and know that I am'. God also had a role in restraining kings and queens – they could be removed if they were deemed to have transgressed. Henry VIII went from being 'defender of the faith' to laying the foundations of the Church of England after the Pope refused to grant him a divorce.

The rebels who became the founding fathers of the United States of America faced a particular problem.

They wanted neither gods nor kings to be the source of their authority. The moment for a renaissance of Athenian democracy had arrived. With every turn, the individual gained greater freedoms and autonomy, and arbitrary powers were reigned in.

Government by the people and for the people underpins what we have come to call liberal democracy. Rules-based systems are neither self-regulating nor self-sustaining. Their vitality and viability depend on participation and commitment.

At least with a god, we knew that there was an answer out there, a truth that could be discovered through discourse and dialogue. This idea is still at the root of much continental Christian socialism as well as the European Union's modus operandi of teleological decision-making. In contrast, the Anglo-Saxon world has put more emphasis on adaptability and resilience.

Monarchs provided a link between God and man, but the belief in their right to govern has become unfashionable as has the hereditary principle. In the last century, there have been some powerful political families like the Chamberlains and the Kennedys, or more recently Bill and Hillary Clinton and Bush father and son, but they don't create enduring dynasties.

Constitutional authority and the control of the military and coercive powers of the state can take a variety of forms. In the UK, we have the king as our head of state. He is also the armed forces' commander-in-chief, even though the prime minister of the day holds the de facto authority. In the US, the president is both head of state and commander-in-chief. The German president is chosen by an electoral college comprising Members of Parliament and electors chosen by state parliaments, and they have limited powers. Deployment of troops, for example, requires an affirmative parliamentary vote.

The military has a special place in our constitutional arrangements. Every five years there is an Armed Forces Act that provides the legal basis for the armed forces and the system of military law. There is an annual vote on the maximum number of personnel to be maintained for service within the armed forces. The deployment of those armed forces is not constitutionally subject to a vote, but any wise prime minister would seek parliamentary endorsement.

Governments are powerful. From deciding on the size and structure of the armed forces and law enforcement agencies to the right to impose taxes, politicians make big decisions. But there are other powerful players who affect our daily lives who are not accountable for what they do. They are the big companies who respond to market forces and consumer choices and in the process collect our data. We buy their products and use their services without giving it a second thought. Occasionally there is outrage when working conditions in a warehouse or some other unfair practice is exposed. But if the service is good and the price is low, most of us continue to buy. And if we don't, unlike a government, the company will cease to exist.

The dot.com revolution in the 1990s heralded the arrival of a completely new form of business, where transactions were carried out over the internet. Amazon, Google, Apple, and Facebook were some of the emerging big players. They generate enormous profits, have global reach, and are difficult to tax. Some of their charismatic owners, who appear to have more power than sovereign leaders, such as Elon Musk, Richard Branson, and Jeff Bezos, have now entered the race to space. We can only dream of governments being as nimble of foot and efficient as they are. We demand safeguards and protection when we hand over personal data to official bodies, but we don't give it a second thought when we deal with the giant tech service providers.

By our own actions we cede power and control to unaccountable organisations in the interest of convenience and efficiency.

The state always plays catch-up, from the expanding powers of the East India Company in the eighteenth century to the use of analytical data by social media companies today. The pace of technological change and innovation vastly outstrips the administrative ability of governments. There are rare moments in times of crisis when the needs of governments and the entrepreneurial capacity of companies combine to produce an outstanding public good in record time, as they did with vaccines during the COVID pandemic, but these moments don't last.

The consumer of the product labelled 'democracy' is getting impatient. Terms such as 'left' and 'right' have lost some of their meaning and become less important.

For many people who want to re-nationalise the railways, it isn't about wanting to return the means of production to the workers. They object to high fares and unreliable services. When the under thirty-fives say they don't believe in the contributory principle, this doesn't mean they don't believe in the mutual support of the welfare state, which includes the retirement pension; they're simply expressing their doubts as to whether there will be anything left in the pot by the time they get to retire. For them, a system of paying for welfare out of current taxation has become unsustainable. But we all love the NHS. Not because it is so ultra-efficient or beyond improvement – far from it. We support the NHS as an institution because it touches our lives, irrespective of age, social status, or income. It responds according to need, and even when the response is inadequate or unreliable, we don't question the underlying philosophy.

The nation state has its roots in providing security for the people. Raising money for a greater collective good – as well as for wars – is what laid the foundations for our system of taxation. In 1799, William Pitt the Younger first levied a direct tax on people's income. It was supposed to be a temporary measure to cover the cost of the Napoleonic Wars, but quickly became permanent. Measures put in place for the safety of the realm thus created the overarching framework for the nation state.

The link between taxation and representation is an old one. It was the rallying cry of the American revolutionaries. To this day, the US collects tax from its citizens wherever they live in the world. Taxes establish the bond between those who govern and those who are being governed. General election manifestos boil down to one thing: 'This is how much money we intend to take from you, and this is what we are going to spend it on.' From education to road building to international aid, all their decisions are part of this basic deal.

There are particular problems in countries whose economies are based on a natural resource like oil. When the wealth of the nation oozes out of the sand, government comes to be about redistributing plenty rather than striking a deal where the government and the governed have a say.

Taxing physical things is relatively easy. But governments are struggling to collect taxes from global corporations and international financial transactions. The latest challenge has come from cryptocurrencies.

The entire system of taxation is based on growth, higher productivity, and increasing output, demand, and revenue.

The ratio of working population to non-working population is changing. Retirement age is going up as is life expectancy, but at nowhere near the same rate. The detrimental impact of economic activity on the global environment is coming close to being irreversible. Growth means using more of the Earth's resources. But cutting back on oil and gas results in less tax revenue. More and more people want increased involvement from the state; these are often the same people who show the greatest concern for environmental sustainability, too often ignoring the correlation between growth, consumption, and the tax revenue necessary to pay for state intervention.

It is the job of democracies to be clear about options and choices and to provide a framework in which decisions about the future can be made.

It will only work if everyone is prepared to participate and accept collective decisions. Not taking an interest is the same as saying 'I don't care about what society I live in'. Waiting to be told what we can and cannot do runs contrary to the essence of democracy. It is wrong to leave it to others to make decisions that have consequences for generations to come. Just as it is wrong to advocate change only for others and assume that we ourselves can continue in our old comfortable ways.

There are many ways of taking part. The ballot box is a good start, though it is about much more than just voting. Other actions may, in the short term, be more effective. But whatever we do, we must demonstrate an awareness of the consequences for others. There is nothing wrong with joining a peaceful Extinction Rebellion demonstration against high-emission air travel. But there is everything wrong with flying first class across the Atlantic to join the demonstration. It is perfectly legitimate to lobby MPs and demand that all social care be free at the point of delivery, but it is not legitimate for MPs to agree with the policy without spelling out that this won't be possible without either raising taxes or making cuts somewhere else.

No politician ever sets out to make the world a worse place, but sometimes what seems progressive and sensible turns out to be the opposite. Confronting unintended consequences is tough.

In 1977 Family Allowance, which consisted of a cash benefit that mainly went to mothers and a child tax allowance that mainly went to fathers, was replaced by Child Benefit. It was a universal benefit that went to the main carer, usually the mother. It was a popular benefit. It was not means tested, embraced every child, and was an investment in our collective future.

In 1988 the chancellor of the exchequer, Nigel Lawson, introduced independent taxation of husbands and wives with the words, 'I propose a major reform in personal taxation, to give married women the same privacy and independence in their tax affairs as everyone else.' As with the introduction of Child Benefit, Lawson's reform was particularly welcomed by women.

In 2013, the coalition government introduced a tax charge that would have to be paid by families containing an adult whose income exceeded £50,000 a year. There was much noise about the actual amounts and perversities in practice, but hardly a whimper about the policy reversal. At a stroke, Child Benefit was no longer universal and independent taxation had gone – and yet today we have one of the most expensive childcare systems in the world.

～

In democracies, we weigh up competing demands and make choices. We rely on the government to use data and information about us to identify areas that require current and future policy intervention. No solution is perfect, and few problems ever go away. We develop new ideas, try them out, dispose of them if they fail, and come up with new ones. We expect decisions to be explained, justified, and defended. Doubt and discussion are essential to progress, but we don't like politicians who admit that they 'don't know'. In this 'trial and error' system of running a society, if things don't work out, we change the government and hope that the new set of politicians will do a better job.

Democracy: The Play

Politics is as much about perception as it is about facts and reality. Popular engagement requires entertainment as well as substance. Little has changed since the last stages of the Roman Republic, when it was said that there were only two things the people anxiously desired: bread and circuses. Today we have the Punch and Judy show that is Prime Minister's Questions.

Like it or not, democracy in action has much in common with theatre. On its political stage you'll find a scene-setting opening, characters and plots, and a conclusion followed by a curtain call. The only difference is that in this play the audience shapes the narrative and has the last word in the last act. Until the next performance, that is.

Sometimes the theatre doesn't matter much. Parliamentary debates range from raucous entertainment to total tedium. They make MPs feel good or bad about themselves and they're a quick way to test the mood of the House, but they rarely make much difference. Televised debates between party leaders on the other hand can make or break a party's election campaign.

The live enactment of *Democracy: The Play* is performed across the globe. Elections provide the stage. Manifestos and ballot papers are the script, candidates and their political parties the players. The final curtain call declares the duly elected representatives, and some of them go on to form the government.

Once the drama of polling day is over, we look forward to the next performance in a few years' time: a revised script, some new players, and possibly a different ending. But it would be a mistake to think that there is nothing to be done until the next season. In this play, it is the audience participation that provides the vitality needed for the system to work. Without it, there is no renewal.

Democracy is about more than putting a cross against a name or party on a ballot paper. It has meaning and purpose. It is about making the idea of government by the people work for the people. It is about sovereignty being held by the people's representatives, who have a duty to protect individual liberty and property within the rule of law.

Elections, voting systems and franchise, political parties, and the constitutional checks and balances that restrain the executive (government) are the building blocks of liberal democracies. Collectively they make up the narrative of the story. Some parts are more visible and exciting than others, but they all matter.

Each society starts with its own history and geography, at varying stages of development. The process of democratic decision-making will present itself in a range of forms. Some good, some bad, but none of them static. Mature and robust democracies can withstand the occasional shock. Over time they have stored up political capital and have become robust and resilient. Some display sliding democratic credentials that cause them to degrade and become hollowed out, whilst others never really take off – their internal tensions and divisions run so deep that the removal of a repressive regime merely results in civil war and chaos.

When I and my fellow members of the House of Commons Foreign Affairs Committee called on the US deputy secretary of defense Paul Wolfowitz, he proudly presented us with a book celebrating the 2005 Afghan parliamentary elections. Despite widespread, sometimes violent, intimidation, there were photographs of women outside polling stations, who had queued for hours, proudly holding up their purple-stained fingers after they had cast their vote. The overall turnout was 50 per cent and women won 28 per cent of the parliamentary seats, more than the 25 per cent required by their constitution. This was a country where illiteracy was estimated to be as high as 85 per cent amongst women and 55 per cent for men. To facilitate voting, candidates were represented by symbols to allow for identification on the ballot. But there were no political parties that represented competing strands of ideas. Instead, there was a long list of individual candidates, voted on by a population that lacked the means of making informed choices. What should have been regarded as an essential first step in the process of building democratic structures was hailed as evidence of success. Job done. Sixteen years later, in August 2021, after heavy losses of life, the United States Armed Forces withdrew from Afghanistan. The Afghan president fled the country, and the returning Taliban took control in Kabul.

Things go wrong when we try to create something without the foundations in place. It is perfectly possible to restore democratic structures or even build them afresh. Germany today is peaceful and economically successful, as is Japan. In 1945 they were aggressors who had been resoundingly defeated. The Allied forces, as victors, did not destroy the civic structures. As best as they could they removed, prosecuted, and punished key offenders. A package of measures ranging from heavy investment in peaceful activities to establishing legal frameworks and constitutional safeguards was put in place. This allowed for elections to be held and governments to be formed. Germany and Japan were being integrated into international organisations, and they in turn accepted the obligations that came with it.

Nation-building that is short term, that destroys existing civic structures and alienates the moderate groups that are key to building a future, is bound to fail. It does not create a demos and a structure that is resilient to internal as well as external threats. Government by the people cannot be imposed on the people without the consent and active participation of the people.

It is also true that the existence of functioning democratic structures does not necessarily prevent dictators from emerging. Adolf Hitler was the leader of a mass movement known as National Socialism. Following a series of electoral successes by the National Socialist German Workers' Party, he was appointed as German chancellor in 1933. The existing powers thought they could control him and his supporters. As it turned out, they were wrong.

The cycle of gaining or losing power, then handing it over or regaining it, begins and ends with elections. And elections start with manifestos, leaflets, and rallies, and end with polling day. Counting the ballot papers is the culmination of a long process of voters making up their minds. The politicians have fought their campaigns and set out their wares, after which the people take sides and decide. We talk of fighting elections for good reason. It is a battle for power. At the end of the day a winner is declared. The losing side consents to the winning side putting its policies into practice and governing. But only until the next time. There will be another election, another chance to change those who hold power. To let the other side have a go. The voters may choose not to do so; they may choose to give the current government another term of office – but they don't have to.

Some practical things have to be in place for the system to work. Like the back of the stage, they don't sound exciting, but they are vital.

Key to it all are political parties. They aren't just labels we attach to a group of similarly minded people. They are important institutions and, in government or in opposition, they make the system work. They can't be created overnight or imposed; they have to evolve and grow out of a society's values and history. Once established they are the gatekeepers, shepherds, and regulators of much of political activity. In government they get a chance to put their ideas and aspirations into practice; when out of government they challenge those in power and aim to come up with better alternatives. At its best the continuous competition to do better creates a society that other nations look to and wish to emulate.

We have taken political parties for granted, and they in turn seem to have forgotten what they are for.

For a democracy to function properly, a society needs clear rules about who is allowed to vote and structures in place to protect the secrecy of the ballot box, prevent voter intimidation, and verify the votes before declaring the final result.

Whether the ballot papers are pieces of paper that are pushed into a box to be counted later, an electronic button that is to be pressed, or a lever to be pulled doesn't really matter. It's a technicality. What does matter is that there are identifiable choices and that if enough people express their preference for one candidate rather than another it has consequences. The larger the majority of the winning side, the more radical they can be.

There is a right to vote, but there is also the right not to vote. Low turnouts, like low audience figures, tell us that people are either not inspired by what is on offer or think the outcome is a foregone conclusion.

The general election in February 1950 had a turnout of 83.9 per cent, the highest of any before or since. Post-war Britain was undergoing dramatic changes, and the people wanted to be part of that change and to have their say. The 2001 general election, which followed the Labour landslide of 1997, had a turnout of just 59.4 per cent. Labour held on to almost all of the seats gained in 1997. Some called it the 'silent landslide', which confirmed the people wanted the government to get on with its programme, while others believed it reflected disillusionment with both sides.

The 2010 general election had a turnout of 65.1 per cent, but no one party had an overall majority. Voters were interested and engaged – they just couldn't make up their minds who should be in charge. I spent most of the 2010 general election campaign on the phone talking to constituents who were not sure who they'd vote for in this election. We used to interpret a response of 'I don't know' as a polite way of saying 'not voting for you'. Not so this time – a great many people quite genuinely had not made up their minds. One woman very perceptively identified the underlying cause: 'You are all saying the same thing, you are just using different words for it.' For her, there was no choice and no alternatives. The main political parties were all just the same.

The 2010 general election resulted in a coalition government between the Conservatives and the Liberal Democrats (or Lib Dems). This was an unusual structure that nevertheless provided five years of stability. The junior coalition partner, the Lib Dems, decided to have a minister in most government departments. Political differences were thrashed out between ministers, and civil servants were left with clear instructions.

Rather than being rewarded for having acted responsibly and having contributed to stable government, in the general election of 2015, the Lib Dems lost forty-nine of their parliamentary seats and were reduced to a rump of eight MPs. Junior coalition partners in other countries tend to take charge of one or two departments, enabling them to go into elections with clear policy achievements. All the Lib Dems could claim was 'just imagine what the Tories would have done if it hadn't been for us'. This didn't seem too much of an achievement to the voters, who gave David Cameron a working majority of twelve. The Lib Dems had done what was right for the country, but they were not given any credit for it in the ballot box.

This was also the general election in which the Scottish National Party (SNP) as good as destroyed Labour in Scotland. They gained fifty seats, thus holding fifty-six of Scotland's fifty-nine parliamentary constituencies.

Voters tend to be more interested in what politicians can offer for the future, rather than displaying gratitude for what has been done in the past. When politicians have no more to give, they are discarded like a lemon that has been squeezed dry. Voters don't have to give a reason or provide a justification; they just put a cross next to a name. And that is how it should be!

There is no perfect voting system. They all have strengths and weaknesses. It's not the most exciting topic of conversation, but it matters. Some systems tend to deliver decisive majorities, while others allow for consensus to emerge.

For general elections, the UK is divided into some 650 parliamentary constituencies. The candidate for each constituency who has the largest number of crosses against their name on the ballot paper is declared the winner. The system is called first-past-the-post (FPTP). All the votes cast for other candidates are of no further consequence.

Other elections in England, Scotland, Wales, and Northern Ireland are held under different systems. Elections for the Welsh Senedd and the Scottish Parliament, for example, use the additional member system, which involves two votes, one for a candidate and one for a party. This introduces an element of proportionality into the outcome as the number of successful candidates reflects the share of the party vote. For the Northern Ireland Assembly, the single transferable vote system is used, which allows for a vote to be transferred to another candidate to make sure it is not wasted.

In 2011, the coalition government held a referendum on replacing Westminster's system of FPTP with the alternative vote system. This would have allowed for voters to rank candidates by preference, but it lacked any element of proportionality. On a voter turnout of 42 per cent, the proposal was rejected by a majority of 67.9 per cent. The referendum was quickly forgotten.

FPTP is more likely to produce a majority government than other systems. Policy trade-offs are struck within the main political parties ahead of elections, rather than being negotiated between parties in coalition agreements after the election. Voters know what the deal is at the time of making their choice.

It is not a voting system chosen by most countries around the world. Post-World War II Germany, for example, opted for the Additional Member System, which requires two votes. One for a candidate and another one for a political party. The size of the German Bundestag varies. Following a general election there are a number of directly elected members of the parliament. If the proportion of votes cast for a political party does not reflect their representation in the Bundestag, additional members are drawn from a party list. The resulting parliament broadly reflects the party-political wishes of the electorate, with some members having a direct constituency mandate and others being dependent on party lists. Some of those rejected by their own voters can return thanks to their political parties. Coalition governments are the norm, as are protracted coalition negotiations. It takes months before the voters know which policies have survived the horse trading and which ones must wait for another day.

The FPTP system gives elected politicians a direct mandate, which establishes a direct link between the Member of Parliament and those entitled to vote.

Proportional systems based on closed party lists break that link entirely and allow the parties to rank candidates. This system was used in the UK for elections for the European Parliament. The half-way house option is a list where the voters rank the candidates.

Pure forms of proportional representation result in a larger number of smaller parties, often with more narrowly defined policy aims. Israel is often cited as the most extreme or purest form of proportional representation.

All this may sound technical and dull, but it fundamentally shapes the nature of the political debate. It determines whether parties can afford to be narrow and selective in their policies or whether they must capture the centre ground in order to succeed. As the core vote that parties can rely on diminishes, the moderate middle – or the floating voter – increases in importance. It's not the most exciting part of the battleground, but it's where most voters make up their minds. Do I have a job, do my children have a place in their local school, and can I get an appointment with my doctor are the questions that matter.

Whatever the electoral system, forming a majority government requires an element of compromise, either within large parties or between a number of smaller ones. It is wrong to think that stable government depends on the voting system. Instability is a reflection of doubt and uncertainty in the minds of the voters. It's just that some systems reflect this more starkly than others. Unstable governments and the absence of governing majorities are testament to divided societies. Liberal democracies should aim to unite rather than divide.

Who is allowed to vote matters as much as how we count the votes. The journey to a universal franchise based on age and citizenship status has been a long one.

The Representation of the People Act of 1918 gave some women the franchise, but it wasn't until the Equal Franchise Act of 1928 that women in England, Scotland, and Wales could vote on the same terms as men. In 1969 the voting age was reduced to eighteen. Nowadays, in a UK general election, anyone on the electoral register in a particular place can cast their vote either in person, by post, or by nominating a proxy. We have done away with making the head of the household responsible for registering voters; that is now done on an individual basis. It is strange to think that this should ever have been contentious.

In the wake of the referendum on our continued membership of the European Union, some young people argued that their vote should have been weighted, counting for more than the vote of a pensioner. The referendum was a significant decision about the future, and they had more future ahead of them.

Of course, there could have been a campaign urging grandparents to hand over their proxy vote to their grandchildren. However, it is unlikely that a system where votes are weighted according to some personal attribute would carry the day. But there *is* pressure for lowering the voting age in general elections to sixteen. They already have the vote for some elections in Wales and Scotland. It is a moot point if this increases voter participation, but there is merit in getting young people into the voting habit whilst they are still in full-time education. This ought to be combined with compulsory teaching about the basics of democracy and how politics works. To educate is to respect the citizens of this country.

Even less glamorous than the subject of voting systems and the franchise is that of the inner workings of political parties. They occasionally hit the headlines when they accept questionable donations or when there is gross internal mismanagement, but for most of the time they are either ignored or taken for granted. And yet, without them, liberal democracy cannot function.

Political parties are more than mere pressure groups – they are membership organisations as well as regulators. For the major parties, the party leader is also a prime minister-in-waiting. Out of government, they manage their grass roots members and prepare for the fight back into power. Being the governing party can put considerable policy restraint on a prime minister and their cabinet, as they have to balance national interest with ideology. Following an election, it's clear that party policy is the same as government policy. Over time these diverge, and developing new policies in preparation for elections, whilst also acting in the collective national interest, becomes more and more problematic. When governments come into power without having had time to reflect and articulate how their ideologies are translated into policy, they fail to renew and become unstable. In recent years we have also seen government formation that has fallen out of kilter with the electoral cycle. This is unsustainable in the long run.

The main parties have a responsibility to absorb some of the more extreme strands on their left or their right. Rather than creating new divisions, they should aim to overcome them. Together with other civic institutions, they are the buffer between dictatorship and mob rule. At their best, they give a clear picture of how the state works and how their policies would change things. Choices are put into context. A party's success or failure reflects not only their internal dynamics but also their part in the political system as a whole.

Without understanding the roots and core philosophies of the competing political parties, it's difficult to make sense of the electoral process. Their evolution over time explains in part why nation-building and establishing liberal democracies is so difficult and takes so long.

Most political parties start with an idea or a grievance. People come together and become a group with common aims and values. Some have their origins in breaking away from an established group over a fundamental policy such as free trade, home rule, or membership of the European Union. Members don't agree on everything, but they broadly share a common view on how society should be organised. They decide who is and is not a member, raise money for the party, and are responsible for complying with electoral law.

Unlike companies and corporations, political parties' internal workings are subject to fewer prescriptive rules and regulations. Beyond ensuring that they comply with the law of the land, and that they are open and transparent about their processes, funding, and the setting up of the Electoral Commission, there is a general reluctance by lawmakers to interfere too much with their internal workings. When things go wrong, sorting them out can be messy, but the balance is probably about right. Though this does not exclude the need to review existing rules and respond to changes in society, such as bringing social media within electoral law.

Some parties have existed for a very long time, some are the result of a merger, whilst others have only brief lives. All of them are more than campaigning organisations. They reach beyond single issues, recognise a collective common good that goes beyond their own interests, and aspire to be part of the process of governing. FPTP makes the emergence of new parties difficult but, as the SNP has shown in Scotland, not impossible. Major parties field candidates in general as well as local elections, but not necessarily in every part of the United Kingdom. Minor ones may choose to only take part in local or parish elections. The legal requirement to put down a deposit before an election as well as the need to formally register a party's name puts some restraint on less serious players entering the field. Parliamentary by-elections are a special case, as they have a habit of attracting a rich variety of colourful candidates.

In the 1994 elections to the European Parliament, the Natural Law Party fielded candidates for all eighty-seven UK seats. This entitled them to televised election broadcasts. One of their manifesto pledges was to maintain the collective health of the country by creating groups of experts dedicated to yogic flying. Out of the 210,000 votes cast in Worcestershire and South Warwickshire, 1,501 were for them. The winning margin of the Conservative candidate was 1,204. As the Labour candidate who came second, I somewhat changed my view on 'minor parties that are amusing but don't make any difference'.

Political parties come and go. Those who survive must adapt and change to remain relevant, and they need to understand the art of internal as well as external party management. They can't just be created overnight in response to a single event. They need a core and a purpose that resonates in the wider population. Even enormous amounts of money can't create and sustain a new political party.

The Labour Party has its roots in organised labour and the trade union movement. Clause IV of the party's constitution committed it to the common ownership of the means of production, distribution, and exchange. Following Labour's fourth consecutive general election defeat in 1992, Tony Blair won the party's leadership contest in 1994 and went through a process of redefining its mission through internal debates and structural organisational changes under the banner of New Labour. The one-member-one-vote method of selecting a leader reduced the power of the trade unions, and all-women shortlists opened up candidate selection for MPs to a more diverse group. Investment in regional organisers and the targeting of constituencies that had to be won to have a governing majority gave strategic focus to campaigning activities. Structural changes, combined with policy development, resulted in the Labour landslide of 1997. The party won 418 seats and had a parliamentary majority of 179, which included an unprecedented number of women MPs.

The Conservative Party, which is the heir to the old Tory Party, can trace its roots back to the formations of conservative associations in the 1830s. It has been the dominant political party in modern British politics. Once known as the Conservative and Unionist Party (still its official name), it has produced three women prime ministers and has historically not been afraid of removing sitting prime ministers once they are deemed to have become an electoral liability. Margaret Thatcher, Theresa May, and Boris Johnson were all forced to resign by their MPs, rather than being ousted by the voters. Liz Truss is the first prime minister to be forced to resign by the markets.

The once mighty Liberal Party has seen its fortunes rise and fall. In 1988 it merged with the Social Democrats, a group of four leading Labour Party figures who had broken away from their party to form a new centre party. Strong at grass roots level, today's Lib Dems are a coalition of economic liberals from the right and social liberals from the left. As a third party, their relative strength tends to depend on the performance of the two main parties. They are challenged by the Green Party for third place.

The Scottish National Party, committed to Scottish independence from Westminster, gained its first parliamentary seat in a by-election in 1967. In 2010 there were six SNP Members of Parliament. They lost the Scottish independence referendum in 2014, but in the 2015 general election they took fifty six of the fifty-nine Scottish parliamentary constituencies represented at Westminster. The most significant loser was the Labour Party. Whilst for some traditional Labour voters Scottish independence was not at the top of their wish list, after seeing a succession of Conservative governments being elected on the back of English votes, they felt it was the only way to get their kind of socialist policies implemented in Scotland.

There seems no obvious challenger to the SNP's dominance of Scottish politics. The call for a new independence referendum combined with a commitment to re-join the European Union implies the rejection of a union with the United Kingdom in favour of a union with the European Union, which isn't quite the same as independence.

One of the UK's most recent new parties was formed in February 2019 when seven MPs left the Labour Party to form the Independent Group. They were joined by three Tory MPs, rebranded themselves as Change UK, and participated in the 2019 European Parliamentary elections, the last before the UK left the EU in January 2020. They captured 3.5 per cent of the national vote. After a fall out in June 2019, only five MPs remained in the party, and after the third and final name change to the Independent Group for Change, the general election of 2019 delivered the fatal blow.

There is nothing static or pre-determined about political parties, nor do they have a right to survive.

Party conferences are public events that rally members and provide a showcase to the world outside. They are a platform for endorsing or rejecting policies and commitments, but the days when the conference itself was the main battleground of ideas have long gone. Broader policy development of the kind necessary to offer voters a comprehensive manifesto package for government requires input from groups beyond membership.

Think tanks take on an important role. For Labour in the 1990s it was the Institute for Public Policy Research, for the Tories in the 2000s, Policy Exchange. For the Lib Dems it was the 2004 collection of essays *The Orange Book: Reclaiming Liberalism* that articulated the new thinking of MPs, many of whom went on to become ministers in the coalition government. Funding think tanks and commissioning research is a very effective way for groups or wealthy individuals to take part in shaping the country's future direction.

The most visible outward representation of a political party is its leader. To be successful they need to project confidence and clarity outwardly and manage the party machinery inwardly. They need to be more forward looking and progressive than the majority of their followers, but not so much that they lose touch. Like metal filings aligning themselves in the forcefield of a magnet.

They need to maintain the support of their core voters as well as being able to reach out to new ones. If they are strong, they surround themselves with people who challenge them and who bring skills to the team that they themselves don't possess. If they are weak, they tolerate only those who agree with them. Keeping all options open and avoiding the creation of divisions is a strength while in opposition, but it is not sufficient in government. Government requires no end of decisions and not all of them will be right. It requires the ability to make mistakes and recover from them. Charisma might get a prime minister elected, but it doesn't necessarily make them an effective leader. They also need luck, or at least the ability to spot and grasp opportunities to make their own luck. A candidate's mettle is tested in leadership contests and elections; character is destiny.

Each party has its own process for electing its leader, but all of them give their MPs a special status in the process. The argument goes that as fellow MPs they know the candidates better, will have worked with them and therefore have a better assessment of their suitability. The general trend over time has been to weaken the role of the MPs – largely making them the gatekeepers of who gets onto the ballot paper – and to strengthen the voice of individual party members. Enhancing membership participation is a good thing, but when the party is in government and the newly elected leader also becomes the new prime minister this system becomes problematic.

Gordon Brown resigned as leader of the Labour Party in 2010 and many assumed that David Miliband would succeed him. His brother's decision to enter the race was seen as audacious but not fatal. To be eligible, an MP required thirty-three of their parliamentary colleagues to sign their nomination papers. With less than an hour before the close of nominations I was asked if I would do David a massive favour and nominate Diane Abbott, as this would ensure a more balanced contest. I politely declined on the basis that I wasn't sure whose reputation would be more damaged: mine, by nominating Diane, or Diane's by having my name on her nomination paper. In the end David Miliband nominated her, and she made it onto the final list of five candidates. The majority of MPs and Members of the European Parliament (MEPs) voted for David, as did the majority of Labour Party members.

David lost to his brother Ed amongst the affiliated members and was ultimately defeated by a majority of 1.4 per cent. By facilitating that a representative of Labour's left, who without his help could not muster the required support in the Parliamentary Labour Party, was on the ballot paper, he split the vote, enabling another candidate, in this case his brother, to defeat him. In 2015, he resigned as leader.

The Parliamentary Labour Party once again achieved a properly balanced ballot by including Jeremy Corbyn, not because they wanted him to win, but because they felt a representative of the left should be included. Over three decades, year after year, he had voted against his own side more often than almost any other MP. Ed Miliband had also introduced a new category of 'registered supporters' and for a mere £3 they too had the right to vote in the leadership contest. Jeremy Corbyn won by a massive majority in 2015. Challenged in 2016 he went into another leadership election, which he won by an even bigger majority. In the general election of 2019 Jeremy Corbyn's Labour Party gained 202 seats, the lowest proportion of seats since 1935.

∿

Leaders matter and so does party discipline. MPs not voting with their own side is the first sign of trouble ahead. The press likes a rebel and a degree of independence of mind is admirable, but it can be destructive. It also means that the party leader has not been able to convince their own side of the strength of their argument. A former Tory chief whip once observed, 'It starts with the frontbench not being willing to compromise with the backbenches. When that happens, you need to be careful, but you can still do something about it. It ends with the backbenches no longer being willing to make compromises with the frontbench. At that point, you've lost.'

Politics is a group activity. We use labels to describe strands of ideas and values. From centre left to moderate right, parties share values and ideas. All parties purport to want to protect the environment, save the NHS, and invest in education; how they do it and how they finance it is what differentiates them from each other. Rather than offer an alternative ideology, their case is often that they would just do it better and more efficiently than the other side. Voting has become transactional and the choice managerial. It is little wonder that voters feel homeless and are tempted to either withhold their vote or go for minor players.

And now we enter the final act of the play.

We have an electoral system; we have a franchise; we have the parties and their manifestos. The leaders and their candidates ask for your vote. Polling day has arrived. All the various strands that shape a liberal democracy have come together. The audience is about to write the final scene in this particular performance.

Or, putting it another way, it is the day when the local representatives of a national franchise give the voters the opportunity to 'buy or sell shares' in the national brand. They decide on what kind of society they want to live in. Do we want more security, property, human rights, and freedom of expression, or would we prefer something more autocratic and prescriptive? Or maybe we just want things to work more efficiently?

Even with FPTP, where the Member of Parliament has the closest and most direct link, the party matters more than the individual. It is not impossible for an independent candidate to win a parliamentary election, but it is very unlikely. When it does happen, it tends to reflect some very specific local circumstances.

This is not to say that the candidate does not matter – they do – just not quite as much as people in general, and candidates in particular, like to think.

~

In 2010 the opinion polls looked bad for Labour, particularly in constituencies gained in the 1997 Blair landslide. Birmingham Edgbaston was one of them. We expected to lose but decided that we wouldn't go down quietly, and that we would fight for every vote. We didn't use national Labour Party material but instead designed our own campaign. We relied on the data and feedback we got from our volunteers. 'I'm Labour, my values are Labour, but I think for myself' was my strapline. Without contradicting Labour's national message, we added a local dimension. We could fall back on years of community engagement, diligent constituency work, reliable voter identification data, and an extensive network of volunteers that reached well beyond party members. The conditions were as good as anyone could hope for. I held on to my seat and became the recipient of *The Spectator*'s 'Survivor of the Year' award. Looking back at the result, we concluded that at best you can withstand a national swing of about 6 per cent. Beyond that, even the best of candidates with the strongest of campaigns will go out with the tide.

Elections, candidates, and political parties are essential building blocks for a functioning democracy, but in themselves they are not sufficient. Politics is and has always been about power, control, and how much freedom the individual can exercise. Power derives from the people, and those who have the authority to exercise power are subject to the constraints of the rule of law. The peaceful handover to the winner after an election is as much part of the daily workings of democracy as is the right of the losers to oppose the policies of the winner, whilst accepting that they have a responsibility to allow the machinery of government to continue.

We don't have state funding for political parties, but taxpayers' money funds the official opposition. In the Commons, so-called Short Money supports the leader of the opposition's office. It is not insubstantial. In 2020–1 the Short Money allocation for Labour was £6.5 million. Smaller amounts are available to the official opposition parties in the House of Lords, known as Cranborne Money.

The concept of His Majesty's Most Loyal Opposition only works because there is a legitimate and realistic expectation that they will get their turn in government. Opposition is not insurgency. It is about challenging the incumbent, and it requires losers' consent.

A lack of losers' consent can lead to severe, even violent, outcomes. There was widespread bewilderment when Donald Trump refused to acknowledge the outcome of the 2020 presidential election. No one anticipated that in January 2021 the US Capitol would be violently attacked by a mob of Trump supporters attempting to overturn his defeat by disrupting the joint session of Congress that would formalise Joe Biden's victory. It was shocking. But the US Constitution and its institutions were stronger than Donald Trump and his insurgents. Joe Biden was duly declared president-elect the following day. A week after the riot, the House of Representatives impeached Donald Trump for incitement of insurrection. More than 500 people were charged with federal crimes. There is an independent commission investigating the attack.

~

Instability in the system and upheavals within government – be it general elections in quick succession or a prime minister being prevented from proroguing parliament by the Supreme Court – reflect an unresolved power struggle between ideas, as recent events have shown. Turbulence in itself is not a sign of failure. It signifies tensions, which a robust democratic system can and should withstand and resolve.

Rules alone do not create political stability. The short-lived Fixed-term Parliaments Act (introduced in 2011 and repealed in 2022) did not prevent three general elections in five years. Replacing the various Acts of Parliament and conventions with a single written, justiciable constitution will not create certainty. It will take the battleground out of Parliament and into the courts, challenging the political independence of the judiciary and how they are appointed.

Press and the media are the fourth pillar of democracy. Holding those in power to account is their democratic duty, but with it come responsibilities. With the rise of social media and the decline in investment in serious journalism, the media too frequently fuels and fosters the kind of damaging populism and misinformation they then go on to condemn.

A free press is essential, but the media collectively is not taking its democratic role sufficiently seriously. When it becomes disruptive and damaging, the calls for curtailing the right to free speech get louder. Who should decide what can and cannot be said on Twitter or TikTok? A regulator, the government, or the companies who own the platform? These are political judgments, but politicians are hesitant to interfere.

We take pride in our history of democratic government and our ability to adapt and change. The classic model of checks and balances is rooted in the separation of powers. The powers are vested in the legislature and the executive, supported by an impartial civil service and the judiciary. Each branch operates within its own boundaries, and they provide a check on each other.

But this model was severely challenged in the wake of the 2016 referendum on our membership of the European Union.

2016–20: The Referendum and its Aftermath

On the morning of 24 June 2016, the resignation of the prime minister was the third item in the BBC news bulletin.

The outcome of the referendum on our membership of the EU was the lead. A majority of the British people had voted to leave. The second item was the fall of the pound to its lowest level against the dollar since 1985.

The referendum result came as an unexpected bombshell to some, whilst for others it was an articulation of something that had been developing over many years: a loss of a sense of identity, belonging, and community. The decision had some obvious immediate consequences, but few anticipated the years of internal strife, upheaval, and bitterness that were to come.

A democratic system based on parliamentary representation and political party groupings found itself faced with divisions that went right across party political lines and a decision that most of the Members of Parliament disagreed with.

The referendum was a nationwide exercise in direct

participatory democracy. A simple binary question, votes counted across the whole of the UK, and a promise by the prime minister that whatever the voters decided, he would implement.

The legislation that paved the way to the referendum did not require a minimum voter turnout or a qualifying majority. A simple majority for a major constitutional question was deemed sufficient. The government, which campaigned for Remain, made no plans for the eventuality of a majority for Leave. The cross-party grouping Vote Leave, which I chaired, was designated by the Electoral Commission to lead the campaign for the opposing side. After the referendum, Vote Leave had no formal role in implementing the outcome.

David Cameron, having promised he would 'do whatever you the voters decide', resigned within hours of the result being declared. The new prime minister, Theresa May, who had also campaigned for Remain, repeated over and over again that 'Brexit means Brexit'. Little effort went into expanding on the precise meaning of that statement. In January 2017, the Supreme Court ruled against the government and confirmed that the process of leaving required an authorising Act of Parliament.

In March 2017, Theresa May triggered Article 50 of the Treaty on European Union, the legal procedure whereby a member state can officially state their intention to withdraw from the EU. It allows for a negotiation period of up to two years, after which the treaty ceases to apply with respect to that member. This was the first time this procedure had been used.

In April 2017, May announced that there would be an early general election in June. She was hoping to increase her slender majority of twelve. Instead, she lost thirteen seats and had to rely on the support of the Democratic Unionist Party (DUP). In July, she introduced a Withdrawal Bill to formally repeal Britain's membership of the EU. MPs succeeded in obtaining a legal guarantee of a vote on any withdrawal agreement. In early 2019, Parliament voted against ratifying the withdrawal agreement three times. The prime minister announced her resignation in May.

Boris Johnson, who had campaigned to Leave, became prime minister in July 2019. In August, on his advice, the queen prorogued Parliament until the State Opening on 14 October. The Supreme Court ruled on 24 September that the government's decision to prorogue parliament for five weeks was unlawful. MPs forced a third request for an extension to Article 50. Parliament refused to approve a revised withdrawal agreement. Three attempts to call an election failed as MPs would not vote to support the process enshrined in the Fixed-term Parliaments Act.

Eventually the Parliamentary General Election Act 2019 was passed, enabling Boris Johnson to call an early general election. The people had not changed their minds about leaving the European Union. The voters broke the deadlock, took back control, and gave Boris Johnson a majority of eighty.

The UK left the European Union on 31 January 2020.

After one referendum, two general elections, three prime ministers, and a Supreme Court ruling that found the prime minister's advice to the queen unlawful, a forty-seven-year long relationship came to an end. Oliver Cromwell might have felt quite at home if he had stepped down from his plinth outside Parliament's St Stephen's entrance. There was something of the Roundheads vs the Cavaliers in this battle.

EU membership had always been contentious. Being a member state of a union requires acknowledging a higher authority than that of the nation state. This is about more than economics; it is about identity, community, and belonging.

The first half of the twentieth century was dominated by two devastating wars, which involved not just Europe but the rest of the world. Millions died and even more were displaced. Empires collapsed. We had to find a way for the continent of Europe in general, and for Germany and France in particular, to live together peacefully.

The UK is and always has been part of European culture, history, and politics. But geography comes before history. As an island nation we always had a choice on how to relate to our neighbours. Did we seek an economic relationship with shared regulatory regimes and trade arrangements, or aim for deeper political union that would ultimately lead to shared laws, taxes, and the creation of a European demos?

The Common Market, founded by the original six of Germany, France, Italy, and the Benelux countries (Belgium, the Netherlands, and Luxembourg), aimed for political union achieved by gradual economic steps of integration. The UK and some other smaller European countries came together in the European Free Trade Area. But in 1973 Britain, Ireland, and Denmark joined the Common Market. We did so for economic reasons. After that, there was no longer a choice for countries on the European continent as to the kind of relationship they wanted with their neighbours. The Common Market became the European Union, with a directly elected parliament. Membership grew to twenty-eight, with other countries hoping to join in due course. The UK shaped some of the significant economic developments, such as the creation of the single market, but always shied away from the big political projects, such as a common currency.

The subject of Europe has divided British politics

on the left as well as the right. It fractured the political parties at different times and for varying reasons. The left, internationalist at heart, was uncomfortable with the dominance of vested corporate interests, but did see workers' rights and equal pay coming from the EU at a time when Margaret Thatcher's government sought confrontation with the trade unions. The right, always more pragmatic about trade and economics, would never accede to the final word over laws and taxes coming from any other place than the nation state.

Harold Wilson called a referendum on our continued membership of the Common Market in 1975. The Social Democratic Party was formed in 1983 as a breakaway from Labour, in opposition to Michael Foot's anti-European stance. Geoffrey Howe's resignation as chancellor of the exchequer over Margaret Thatcher's policy on European Monetary Union in 1990 triggered the events that led to her resignation.

John Major's premiership was bedevilled by infighting over the Maastricht Treaty. In 1992, he negotiated opt-outs for the UK, primarily that we would not be under any obligation to join the single currency.

Tony Blair was the first British prime minister who supported EU membership for geopolitical strategic reasons and was prepared to fully engage at all levels to shape the institution's future direction.

∾

I met the prime minister before Christmas in 2002. Tony Blair wanted to get the representatives on the Convention on the Future of Europe to agree to the creation of a president of the European Council. The position was designed to create continuity of leadership in the institution that represented the member states. The presidency of the Council changed every six months, whilst the Commission and the European Parliament were in post for four years. As a member of the Praesidium of the Convention, the steering group under the leadership of the former French president Valéry Giscard d'Estaing, I was involved in many of the early discussions. I was there as a representative of the UK Parliament, not government, but we worked closely together. Blair argued that the agreement to create this new role was the most significant decision facing us. When I suggested that maybe the invasion of Iraq might be more important, he countered that events in Iraq would unfold now, whatever we decided – but that we could, and must, shape what happened in Europe.

The US-led invasion of Iraq in 2003 was supported by the UK, Australia, and Poland, but neither France nor Germany joined. The position of president of the European Council was created, but as events unfolded,

British focus and energy drifted away from the EU to other matters.

~

The Treaty of Lisbon recognised the European Council as an EU institution and included other significant constitutional matters. In 2007 Gordon Brown signed the Treaty, but rather than joining other national leaders and heads of government, he decided to do so later the same day, on his own.

David Cameron was equally reluctant to engage with the EU. In his leader's speech in Bournemouth in 2006, he chastised his party: 'While parents worried about childcare, getting the kids to school, balancing work and family life – we were banging on about Europe.' As prime minister, he hoped that by not talking about it, the problem would just go away. But in the 2014 European Parliament election, the United Kingdom Independence Party (UKIP) gained more MEPs than any other party. The rise of Nigel Farage's UKIP was as big a threat to the Conservative Party in England as the success of the SNP was to Labour in Scotland. In the 2015 general election, UKIP had the third largest popular vote, ahead of the Lib Dems. In 2016, Cameron called the referendum that triggered his resignation.

≈

Leaving the European Union was probably always going to be protracted, contentious, and divisive. While the treaties provided a legal basis for leaving, there wasn't a road map. But there are some lessons from those four years that we should learn from and not forget.

With every ballot there is one side that wins and another side that loses. Casting a vote is the process by which it is established which side carries more weight. Leave had a majority of 3.8 per cent on a turnout of 72 per cent. That is a clear majority on a high turnout. Even when an outcome is far from what most people expected, it should be respected. But that is not what happened. Whole swathes of the country who voted Leave were denounced as being old, stupid, or racist, or all of the above.

Normally we would have expected the governing party and the opposition to have negotiated a new consensus. But the institutions at home ceased to function, and abroad the government was outmanoeuvred by the EU.

The European Union was determined to make leaving difficult and focused on the problems created by land borders. That was a perfectly rational and logical position for them to take. They did not want to pave the way for other countries to follow the UK.

The UK was not prepared for this. Abroad, the unity of the EU did not fracture, and at home 'losers' consent', something that has always been taken for granted in our constitutional arrangements, was not forthcoming.

Parliament, having set the terms for the referendum, refused to accept the outcome. The focus was on bringing about a second referendum. A similar message went to European partners. Some argued that it was a mistake to hold a constitutional referendum on a simple majority, and yet the legislation had been agreed by all sides.

We can't always get what we want, but as long as there is faith in the process, we accept compromise. And yet on this occasion the very people who had set up and designed the process refused to respect the result. Rather than trying to understand the reasons why people voted the way they did, they demanded it be reversed. Democracy as a system collapses when politicians despise the people whose vote they rely on. Unlike the politicians, the voters remained steadfast throughout.

Where precisely sovereignty lies and who exercises it at any given moment is a moot legal as well as political point. In the UK, the legal sovereign is 'the Crown in Parliament'. In the 1970s, the then prime minister Edward Heath deliberately spoke little about sovereignty. Common Market membership and the referendum was said to be all about economic prosperity. This was a conscious decision taken by the politicians in charge at the time. The strategy worked in the referendum in 1975 but failed in 2016.

The UK's relationship with the European continent has been a repeated failure of democratic accountability at national level. In 2019, the House of Commons attempted to claim sovereignty for itself by refusing to allow the referendum result to be implemented. It was not until later that year that the entity that ultimately holds sovereignty in a democracy – the people – reasserted their claim in the general election.

In the wake of the Brexit vote, it is the use of referendums that requires the most serious reflection. Some countries like Germany don't allow nationwide referendums, whilst others like Switzerland have sophisticated and long-established mechanisms for holding them.

There are some powerful arguments for moving from representative democracy to direct participatory democracy on matters of constitutional significance or moral/ethical issues that transcend party politics.

Only three national referendums have been held across the whole of the UK: on the Common Market in 1975, on the Alternative Vote in 2011, and on EU membership in 2016.

There have been local referendums on a number of issues, from giving devolved powers to the North

East, to whether there should be a Greater London Authority composed of a directly elected mayor and a London Assembly. The Welsh people had their say on the law-making powers of the National Assembly. A pre-legislative referendum was held in Scotland over whether there was support for the creation of a Scottish parliament with devolved powers, and whether the parliament should have tax-varying powers. Some of them were carried, others were not.

Voters expect some consistency and purpose when they are asked to make a decision – not a random process or one that is used as a last resort when politicians can't resolve a problem.

There is no logic in asking the people of Birmingham whether they want a directly elected mayor and, when they say no, imposing a directly elected mayor of the West Midlands Combined Authority – and yet this is exactly what happened after the English mayoral referendums in 2012.

There was no referendum on directly elected Police and Crime Commissioners, even though their creation – and with it another layer of administration – was supposed to make the police answerable to the communities they serve.

The 2014 Scottish Independence Referendum asked voters, 'Should Scotland be an independent country?'

Fifty-five per cent said no and 45 per cent said yes on an 85 per cent voter turnout. All sides referred to it as a 'once in a lifetime opportunity'. The SNP is now calling for another referendum arguing that, as Scotland voted to remain in the EU, the situation has sufficiently changed for another plebiscite to be right and proper. They will have to make the case for leaving the Union of the United Kingdom in order to join the European Union. Rather than independence as it is commonly understood, it is about the membership, and obligations, of a different union.

Parliament would do well to agree on the key principles that underpin the circumstances when a referendum of any kind is called and define some of the parameters. It is perfectly possible to have two-stage referendums: first on the principle and second on the details of implementation. But if this is the case, then the terms of both have to be clearly spelt out in advance. Asking for another vote because the first one did not deliver the desired outcome is not legitimate.

Other countries conduct referendums after extensive public consultation and debate that involves civil society and local communities. The Irish referendums on legalising same-sex marriage and abortion are good examples of arriving at a consensus on contentious moral questions.

There should be clear choices and clear consequences, and those who lead the campaigns for either side must have a responsibility for, or be part of the implementation of, the outcome.

There was a good case for a referendum on the Lisbon Treaty. It brought about significant changes, including more qualified majority voting. The consequences of the vote would have been clear: change or the status quo. All three main parties promised a referendum in the run-up to the 2005 general election. But we didn't have one as it no longer suited the main players to 'ask the people'. The heat generated in the run-up to the general election had gone out of the fight.

The most lasting legacy of both the Scottish independence and the Brexit referendums has been the absence of losers' consent, the failure to respect the majority view. In both instances, the refusal to accept the outcome morphed into an expression of moral superiority by the minority. Political debate gave way to abuse. The battle for the centre ground, the main feature of general elections, is almost impossible in binary referendums. Social media allowed for this polarisation of views to become more visible and more noisily articulated, but the roots are deeper. The country became divided between 'good people' who voted to remain and 'bad people' who voted to leave. Discussions and dialogue gave way to exchanges of assertions. 'I disagree' became 'you are lying'. These divisions will have to be healed, but it will take some time.

The years between 2016 and 2019 did not just trigger a constitutional crisis; they were a moment when the people of these islands made a fundamental decision about how they are governed. It was a decision about identity, community, and belonging rather than economic wellbeing. Some things have been resolved; others are still the matter of intense negotiations.

Mainland Europe will not become a modern-day empire as some have suggested. Geography plays an important part, as it shapes a country's history. There will continue to be different models of how the nations of the European continent relate to each other. Membership of the single currency, the euro, will require deeper political integration. It is not a foregone conclusion that in time all EU member states will join. At the time of the referendum, the EU was not willing to contemplate an institutional architecture that would have allowed for two kinds of membership – euro and non-euro – as a permanent arrangement. Opt-outs were useful but not sufficient to resolve the British public's unease of being part of what was a political project. In years to come, our decision to join the Common Market in 1973 will be seen as more remarkable than our decision to leave the European Union in 2016.

There may yet be another chapter to be written on what this has done to the Conservative Party. The questions of free trade, tariffs, and Irish Home Rule tore apart political parties in the nineteenth century. The long-term consequences of the battle over our place in the political structures of the European continent and globalisation may yet have similar consequences in the twenty-first century.

What Next for Democracy?

Those who predicted in the latter part of the last century that humanity's political evolution was complete and that the universalisation of Western liberal democracy as the final and perfect form of human government had been achieved, were wrong.

We had assumed that building nations, changing regimes, and creating the conditions for democracy to flourish could be done overnight. Bitter experience has made us scale back our ambitions. We try to manage failed and failing states and attempt to hold aggressors at bay. Rather than hoping to remove autocracies and dictatorships, we decided to build trade relationships – what the Germans called 'Wandel durch Handel', or change through trade. Russia's invasion of Ukraine ended that hope. Democracies are waking up to the uncomfortable truth that co-existence with dictatorships doesn't work, and that democracies have to fight for their place in the world order if they want to survive. A country that does not respect the rights of its own citizens will not respect the rights of its neighbours.

Liberalism, based on the belief of the autonomous individual, has not prevailed. There is no hegemony for a single kind of identity. By condemning those who want respect for their identities, we fuel populism and create division.

The challenges at home and abroad are real. We must not settle for a managed decline of democracy but accept individual responsibility for renewing those elements that have fallen into disrepair. Rules-based systems are neither self-regulating nor self-renewing. Their vitality and legitimacy do not spring from supranational institutions but from the daily interactions of every single one of us.

∼

In 431 BC, the Athenian statesman Pericles delivered an oration at the funeral of the first Athenian soldiers to lose their lives in the Peloponnesian War. His speech was reported by the Greek historian Thucydides.

> Our administration favours the many instead of the few; that's why it is called a democracy. The laws afford equal justice to all alike in their private disputes. An Athenian citizen does not neglect public affairs when attending to his private business. We consider a man who takes no interest in the state not

as harmless but as useless and although only a few may originate a policy, we are all able to judge it.

This roughly translates into, 'Not being interested in politics means you don't care about what kind of society you live in, and this isn't something to be proud of.'

Democracy is precious and can be robust, withstanding a degree of turbulence, but it is also a living thing that requires nurture and renewal. When we become complacent and degrade the system, its powers wane and ultimately fail. Above all, it is not a spectator sport. Its vitality depends on participation, and it needs to be contested to thrive.

How we arrive at a decision is as important as the decision itself. In the absence of coercive powers, consensus, trust, and goodwill have to be achieved by persuasion. This is messy and can be time-consuming, but it is infinitely better than any alternative.

In 2015, the Birmingham University Students' Union organised election hustings. Candidates across several constituencies from the Labour Party, Conservatives, Lib Dems, UKIP, and the Green Party took part. Unlike the lively, sometimes bruising encounters from the past, the evening was sedate, almost dull. There was a minor ripple of excitement when the UKIP candidate advocated zero per cent VAT on tampons and other sanitary products. It did not last. Cheering UKIP didn't suit the room, even though the students liked the policy.

As I was leaving the hall, a student bemoaned that no one on the platform had been outrageous or controversial. I suggested that maybe the questions hadn't been challenging. She looked bewildered. Wasn't it the candidates' job to be inspiring, radical, and contentious? I almost replied that you can't just outsource outrage but decided that now was not the time to make new enemies. But she had a point. Rather than igniting debate with our daring visions of the future, all we aspired to was not causing offence.

Democracy requires a demos with a physical and geographical base, centring around social and intellectual communities. Civil society, the third sector, think tanks, trade unions, churches, schools, universities, hospitals – they all form part of that fabric. Communities are where new ideas are generated, alternative policies developed, and movements mobilised. Change can be unsettling and disruptive. It's easier to advocate change for others when we believe we don't have to give up anything ourselves. Without constructive engagement, there is no lasting change and no reform.

∼

Political parties are a critical part of the democratic infrastructure. They take care of organisational and administrative processes and create a broad framework for shaping political thinking. They turn ideas and aspirations about what kind of society we want to live in into a programme for government. Election manifestos provide the parameters. They spell out priorities and hopes, options and compromises, as well as overcoming apprehensions and containing fears.

Party conferences are the occasion when they open the windows of their internal workings to the outside world. Who decides what, where the money comes from, and who sits at the table says a lot about the character of a political organisation.

~

Election campaigns are not only about making promises for the future, but also containing fears from the past.

In 1992, the polls had predicted an end to Labour's thirteen years in opposition. In their campaign, the Tories focused on Labour's past economic performance. The poster of a set of boxer's gloves with the words 'Labour's double whammy of more taxes and higher prices' said it all. Despite a poor showing in the polls in the early stages, John Major and the Conservatives won a fourth term.

Labour's 1997 general election campaign included a pledge card with five relatively modest promises. The promises to reduce class sizes in schools and NHS waiting lists, speed up the criminal justice system, and get more young people off benefits and into work were all about the future. The promises not to increase income tax rates, cut VAT on heating, and keep interest rates and inflation as low as possible were responding to fears from the past.

In this election, Labour ended its eighteen-year spell in opposition, winning a parliamentary majority of 179. Nationally it was a landslide, but not so in Winchester.

The Conservative Gerry Malone had won his Winchester constituency in 1992 with a majority of 8,121. In 1997 he lost to the Lib Dems' Mark Oaten by two votes. It was reported that neither Malone nor his wife had been registered to vote in Winchester. Having later identified a procedural error by the returning officer, Malone went to court, challenging the result. The judges ordered a rerun. In the by-election six months later, Mark Oaten increased his majority from 2 to 21,556.

The Tories did not regain the seat until 2015. Voters hate nothing more than a bad loser.

≈

The major parties are struggling with declining and ageing memberships. They resort to making bargain offers such as, 'Join us today at a one-off rate of £3 and you too can have a vote in our leadership contest'. This kind of transactional pitch isn't wrong, but it is insufficient to create a sustainable, representative membership base.

With FPTP, everything has its beginning and its end in the constituency. It is the Member of Parliament's source of legitimacy and the geographical unit for candidate selection, membership activity, and campaigning. Keeping a local party active and engaged can be hard work. Where the incumbent has a large majority, the outcome in the general election is a foregone conclusion, so the small number of party activists who have a vote in the candidate selection effectively choose the next MP. Where there is little hope of victory, raising money and recruiting volunteers is tough.

Open primaries – voting rounds that allow anyone, even non-party members, to choose a particular party's parliamentary candidate – have been a route to Westminster for a handful of MPs. The idea of widening the base for selection beyond party members has lost much of its initial appeal, after some of those elected turned out to be just that bit too independent for party managers.

The decision to join a political party involves taking sides. In some ways it is not unlike supporting a football team, but it is about more than just a sense of belonging, community, and identity. It is a choice based on ideas and values and goes much wider than geography, demographics, or ethnicity. Without values, politics descends into little more than pitting the strength of one group against that of another.

People have always cared about the things that affect them and their families; they just find it increasingly difficult to match their set of values and concerns with a particular political party. It is no longer just about class, workers and their bosses, progressives and conservatives, or interventionists and free marketeers. Political parties have always been a broad coalition of views, but today's groupings just don't quite match voters' expectations any more.

Parties must be election-winning organisations, but without values they become empty vessels. Few of the big challenges – such as the environment, the intergenerational imbalance, or geographical concentration of wealth – are addressed in ways that inspire confidence in the future. If we can't articulate what we are for, we end up defining ourselves by what we are against.

∼

There is an implicit deal. We know that for public services to be provided we have to pay taxes, but we don't much like doing it. We understand that putting on a seat belt or sticking to speed limits is in our own interest, but we still need the law to force us to do it. In exchange for being made to do things we don't much like, government allows us to believe that there are painless quick fixes.

Climate change is a good example. Dealing with humankind's damage to the global environment will require substantially more adjustments than just banning plastic carrier bags and disposable plastic cutlery. Science will partly come to the rescue, as it did during the pandemic, but it won't solve all the problems. Hoping that others will change is not enough. Each and every one of us will have to change the way we work, live, and do business. We know this to be true, but we don't like those who tell us so.

Government by the people and for the people needs to do better. Democracy is as much about having the freedom to make choices and asserting rights as it is about accepting responsibilities. There is no way round it: actions have consequences.

Based on today we make decisions about tomorrow and the day after tomorrow. Facts about the future are scarce, and people's choices and preferences are neither rational nor predictable.

For democracy to work, there has to be trust and the system has to be able and willing to change and adapt.

Trust is fostered by accountability, transparency, and predictability; providing solutions to specific problems also helps. Most of the problems will recur, and none of the solutions will be perfect. That is implicit in the human condition. No one group of people will always be right. All those involved in shaping and implementing policy must have the courage to ask themselves and others inconvenient questions. Checks and balances prevent excesses. Laws and rules constrain and provide a degree of certainty and predictability. All this takes time and appears painfully inefficient.

Tony Blair and New Labour were accused of wanting to create a technocratic party that was free from control by its membership. Jeremy Corbyn's Labour went to the other extreme, aspiring to be a vibrant movement with little appetite for shouldering the responsibilities of government.

There is a world of difference between party policy that, on the one hand, remains anchored in core values and priorities and, on the other hand, is designed and shaped by focus groups.

Once in government it's easy to forget party members. Ministers have wider responsibilities. What the party wants and what is right for the country will not always be the same. These tensions are inherent in our system. They need to be managed, not ignored. Party chairs used to be powerful figures with a seat at the Cabinet table.

Today, they are more likely to be 'ministers without port-folio' and general fixers.

~

Democracy has always been in some sort of crisis. There has never been a golden age when leaders were wise and selfless, institutions trusted and impartial, and the people lived in the best of all possible worlds. We ideal-ise the past, are complacent about the present, and don't think enough about the future.

Democracy is a system of trial and error; it is con-tested. Whenever things get tough, we jump to conclu-sions, condemn those we disagree with, and don't reflect on whether we are the ones responsible for having created the conditions that allowed for things to go wrong.

Those who were surprised when Donald Trump won the 2016 presidential election were stunned when in 2020 over seventy-four million Americans voted for him again. Joe Biden may have defeated him, but it was hardly a triumph for democracy that the political system of the most eco-nomically successful democracy in the world could only offer a choice of two white, male septuagenarians. Rather than being outraged by Trump's success, we should ask why there isn't a wider and more diverse field of people willing and able to enter the presidential race.

Democracy as a global system is on the wane. There was a time when we thought that China and Russia would become like 'us'. The internal power struggles and jostling for position in the Communist Party and the Politburo were not comparable to free elections, but they did result in leaders being deposed. Yet in 2022, neither Russia's President Putin nor China's Chairman Xi Jinping show any signs of being prepared to share power with anyone.

The economic supremacy of the West is being challenged by emerging powerful players in the Indo-Pacific and by China's relentless mercantile approach to foreign policy, driven by gaining strategic access to natural resources and markets. Russia is not just an effective disruptor but, as the war with Ukraine has shown, also a brutal aggressor. Existing nuclear powers like Pakistan, and aspiring ones like Iran, contribute to the potential for global instability.

The World Wide Web started as a system designed for everyone. It opened up access to, and the exchange of, data and information. Today it is difficult to keep up with the development of computer devices, software, and functions. What started with numerous small entrepreneurial teams is now dominated by a handful of global players. As they control the innovation, they also control the rules.

Digital technology and open access to data can bring about transparency and innovation, but in the wrong hands it facilitates repression and surveillance. When the Chinese government demands 'cyber sovereignty' it asserts absolute sovereignty reinforced by censorship and bans. Like all authoritarian regimes, it attempts to ensure stability by preventing dissent from within and without. Digital authoritarians build closed systems protected by absolute views.

A free and open cyberspace requires internet governance and the right kind of norms of behaviour agreed at an international level. The current, relatively small cadre of professionals who safeguard the technical standards on which cyberspace operates are overwhelmingly from or operating in democratic nations. But representation will diversify with the influx of a new cadres of technical professionals.

Domestic data localisation laws pose a new challenge; some impose entirely different criteria upon foreign businesses operating within their countries. Russia claims sovereignty over the data of Russian citizens no matter where that citizen is or where their data was created. It imposes a legal requirement on all domestic and foreign companies to accumulate, store, and process personal information on Russian citizens on servers located within Russia's borders.

Liberal democracies face a dilemma. They want to defend the freedom of speech and enterprise, whilst acknowledging the duty to protect their citizens. The right to privacy and ownership of personal data is precious. We demand safeguards and put constraints on our governments, and yet in the interest of convenience we happily hand over masses of personal data to companies. This doesn't just distort how markets work – it also plays into the hands of hostile states, disruptors, and criminals.

Technology was designed to be a great leveller but has rapidly become an oligopoly of global private companies, difficult to regulate and almost impossible to tax. We thus deal with sovereign individuals as well as sovereign states.

~

Technically it would be perfectly possible to replace votes in Parliament with votes by the public – that is, to have direct participatory democracy rather than our clunky, ponderous representative democracy.

An issue such as whether the state pension should be more protected than other benefits could be put to a direct vote. Rather than leaving it to MPs, we could ask the public: 'Should the triple lock for pensioners – where the basic state pension will rise by a minimum of

2.5 per cent, the rate of inflation, or average earnings, whichever is the largest, continue?'

Dial 333 for 'Yes' and 555 for 'No'.

As pensions are also about intergenerational fairness, we could devise a system of weighting votes in accordance with age. No ballot would be accepted until a 50 per cent turnout had been reached. As this law would apply to the whole of the UK, we would require a majority in England, Scotland, Wales, and Northern Ireland. Anyone with a National Insurance number could participate.

Undeniably such a ballot would capture the mood of the people more accurately than a vote in Parliament. But what it lacks is coherence and values. It does not weigh up competing demands and resource allocation. It does not make the link between raising taxes and spending them. It would be difficult to rally public enthusiasm on issues such as improving prisons, supporting asylum seekers, or constructing new sewers. Socially progressive legislation, like the Civil Partnership Act 2004, would be even more difficult. On the other hand, anything to do with animals would have an easier time.

Politicians would be relieved of their responsibilities; indeed, they'd be redundant, only to be replaced by administrators. Even under a system of direct participatory democracy, there would still have to be someone who decides what questions to ask and when to ask them, but this time without constraints, accountability, or responsibility.

∾

Today's society is more interconnected than any before it and faces problems that can only be resolved on a global level. And yet we still relate most readily to our neighbourhoods and things that we experience directly. We need a reason for holding together and sharing what we have that goes beyond the here and now.

Those able to manage and interpret, analyse, and synthesize the mass of data and information generated, some of it in real time, will hold the levers of power.

We always look to science and technology for solutions. From Prometheus to Albert Einstein, new insights, discoveries, and inventions drive progress and open up opportunities as well as creating new threats.

Today's technological advances outpace our individual ability to comprehend and government's capacity to control. They are changing how we behave and react and not all of it for the better. This does not mean that traditional ideologies are inadequate, that technology effaces politics, and that democratic decision-makers should be replaced by administrators of technological solutions.

Technology is likely to intensify rather than reduce social divides. Increasingly, the moral questions will be about when not to act. Resisting the urge to do something, when we can, is hard. From genetic engineering to medically assisted suicide, we are moving from the technical and ideological to the moral and ethical. We will need to change the way we frame debates. What passes for the 'right answer' will depend on the values we hold.

Debates on values require direct human interaction that establishes mutual trust. In 2015 a Private Members' Bill on Assisted Dying was introduced in the House of Commons. The Birmingham Edgbaston constituency has a high number of doctors, nurses, and healthcare workers. It has some very active churches and the Catholic Oratory nearby. I had my own views on the subject, which I had not articulated in public. I wanted to hear what people thought as well as test my own arguments.

I took part in three public meetings. One convened by medics, one organised by the churches, and the third open to constituents. We started with a lawyer explaining the provisions of the bill. The meetings needed hardly any input from the chair. The comments were thoughtful and respectful. Whether people changed their minds is a moot point, but I doubt that anyone went home without having taken in some point that had not occurred to them before. We didn't agree on how I should cast my vote, and I had not offered to be mandated, but we had a shared understanding of how I would arrive at my decision.

In 2008 the global financial systems came close to total collapse. This wasn't brought about by some external attack or a single event but by the accumulation of a series of individual decisions, within a system so complex that no one institution or government had the complete picture. The fallout was massive. When the queen visited the London Stock Exchange in 2008, she asked why economists had failed to foresee something so big. Eight months later she received an answer by letter. It amounted to a lot of very bright people, in the UK and abroad, whilst doing their own jobs well, lacking the collective imagination to see how a series of interconnected imbalances over which no single authority had jurisdiction would destabilise the whole system and put the entire global financial system at risk.

There is nothing novel in seeing only part of the picture and failing to anticipate the overall impact; it's just that today things happen so much more quickly and the consequences of anything going wrong are so much more far-reaching.

No one system or structure can control things for ever, but liberal democracies have to become more responsive to the new challenges. Resilience is based on openness, free exchange of verifiable data and information, and the acceptance that sometimes things will go wrong. Learning how to fail and do so quickly is something we can learn from successful entrepreneurs. In the absence of a perfect way of running society, there has to be room for trial, error, and doubt.

Neither democracy nor our politics is broken, but there is a sense of disillusionment. Big companies provide better services than the state. Voters no longer take decisions on trust or accept that government knows best. They aren't saying that autocracies are better at solving problems; they just want their governments to be more responsive, more nimble, and more competent.

It matters where decisions are made. Wales, Northern Ireland, Scotland, Greater London, and some regional mayors have acquired greater powers. But this hasn't been the case across the United Kingdom, and the problem is most acute in England.

Part-time regional ministers and Regional Select Committees had a brief life during Gordon Brown's premiership, but they came to an end during the coalition government. The Government Offices for the English Regions, which had officially devolved functions, met the same fate, as did the regional development agencies. The newly created local enterprise partnerships were a patchy and inadequate substitute. Some cities decided to have directly elected mayors. In other areas, local authorities came together and opted for metro mayors. In the absence of English regional government, there was a case for allowing a new system to evolve rather than be imposed. The new arrangements have not created new, independent income streams. This is unfinished business.

The question of 'who speaks for England outside London' remains unanswered. For much of our island's history it may not have mattered much, but it matters now.

As we leave one union, the European Union, we must ensure the cohesion of the other, older union: the Union of the United Kingdom and Northern Ireland.

The United Kingdom Union, forged and formed over centuries, is bound together by geography, common history, and shared institutions. Wales, Scotland, Northern Ireland, and England each have a unique contribution to make. We share a monarch, a currency, an army, and a parliament.

Democracy is about giving cohesion and purpose to a society. If all it needed was more data and efficient administration, we would just hand it over to 'Government Inc.' and have done with it. But government in a democracy isn't like running a business. It's about continuously finding partial solutions to recurring problems. When things go wrong, it can't declare itself insolvent and start all over again. It can't represent only a narrow segment of society and ignore the rest. It operates by consent and is driven by values, not profits.

At its core, the machinery of government has to prevent tyranny while still ensuring that something happens. Navigating these competing demands is a never-ending battle, and there are never right or wrong answers.

The opposition will be outraged by administrative incompetence. Mutterings of 'too late, too early, too much, not enough' will always be with us. Campaigning slogans are essential for elections. But there comes a moment when an alternative must be offered. The competing claims for the right to govern, underpinned by values that are articulated, contested, and defended, are put to the test in an election.

Respect for institutions is what makes democracies resilient. We may not like the people in charge at any given time, but we respect what they are trying to do, and we know how to bring about change.

We cannot demand that our leaders be people 'just like us' and then express shock and horror when they turn out to be 'just like us', with flaws and weaknesses. But we can and must expect that, when they are in positions of power and responsibility, they put our interests first. If they don't, we remove them.

Democracy is about government by the people and for the people. That means that the buck stops with us, the people. We voted governments in, and we can vote them out.

We know that we don't know what tomorrow will look like. Today is not the best of all possible worlds. We don't have all the answers, but the next generation has the right to expect to be given a fair chance to make decisions about their lives, the way we were. They will make mistakes, just as we have.

What we do and how we do it is not up to somebody else, it's up to every single one of us. Democracy is not a spectator sport. Its vitality and life force demand participation. That is exciting and invigorating; it is also very scary.

We are the people. Our actions shape the future, and that is democracy.